Coast Guard Beach, Eastham   SANDFLATS AND STARFISH   October 3, 1990 – 5:35 pm

COASTAL EFFECTS

CAPE COD, MARTHA'S VINEYARD & NANTUCKET

PHOTOGRAPHY AND ESSAYS BY

JON VAUGHAN

PUBLISHED BY
YANKEE INGENUITY
CHATHAM, MA

IN MEMORY OF LYNNE

COASTAL EFFECTS

COASTAL EFFECTS is the catchall phrase used by frustrated forecasters to excuse their inability to predict the peculiar weather conditions common to Cape Cod, Martha's Vineyard and Nantucket. Stranded in water, these ancient shifting sand spits and dunes are little more than ripped remnants of an eroding coastline bounded by a great continent and an even greater ocean. This location is dynamic and so is the weather. The confluence of conflicting currents, air and water, enhanced by disparate temperatures confounds even the best forecasters.

Unpredictability is so great that most natives must rely on joint aches and avian agitation to determine daily weather trends. The seemingly dismissive advice, *If you don't like the weather, just wait five minutes* is not a rude joke, it is reality. The corollary, *If you don't like the weather, just go to the next town* is also true. Though the climate is temperate, the weather is temperamental, both a blessing and a challenge to all who live here. Dramatic or dreary, splendid or dismal, it is the main subject of brief encounters. Past storms are always compared to recent ones. The best ones increase in size, intensity and duration with each recitation.

I particularly like the coastal fog which many morning forecasters tell you will burn off by noon, and then it lingers until last light. Sometimes, rain follows the fog, soaking the landscape, saturating the colors of the sand, grass, leaves and lichens. The enriched hues are momentary, disappearing with a fresh breeze. When the wind whips up into a gale or hurricane, the Coast Guard flies flags to warn mariners. Like seagulls following a fishing fleet, people flock to the water's edge to watch the waves pound the beach. If the tide is high, the damage is severe. Boats break from their moorings. Piers, houses and shoreline succumb to the surf. After the storm subsides and the tide ebbs, the sand flats reappear, sculpted into serpentine ridges as if raked by a Zen gardener.

When calm returns, the still waters reflect a changeable sky. Backlit by the setting sun, clouds, tidal pools, silhouetted sand bars, random rocks, piers and boats create mesmerizing rorshach patterns that darken and disappear with nightfall. Simultaneously, in the eastern sky, the moon appears on the horizon like a giant gold doubloon salvaged from the deep blue. A bright path of shimmering light floats to the shore on liquid ripples. Walking off the beach you notice your night shadow and are thankful for a lunar lit path.

When you are encompassed by a coastline, your way of life is dramatically influenced by the sea and its coastal effects. You depend upon the ocean's bounty and beauty for life and peace of mind. You respect its force for survival and its magnitude with humility. You bear witness to human and animal efforts to live on its edge. You know the water is at all points of the compass. You are drawn to it daily as if the horizon were a magnet. The closer you come, the more you sense its effects. Saltwater, seaweed and sand flats are smelled before seen. *Weathered* is the natural state of being. Erosion is the natural course of events. Boats and barriers abound, both seaworthy and seabeaten. Shoes and socks are abandoned for a barefoot massage in sand and surf. Beaches and rocks are windswept and water worn, baked and bathed by sun and tides. The tides tie you to the cycles of the moon. The winds tie you to the rhythm of the waves. Life and love tie you to the magic of the place.

It is the magic of the place that inspires me to photograph. My love for the place compels me to share it. My respect for the place obliges me to protect it. It is my hope for the place – *the Cape and Islands* – that these photographs will honor and help preserve it.

To best represent the coast and its effects I have artificially sequenced the photographs by day of the year while disregarding chronology by year. Starting with January and progressing month by month, the commonalities and idiosyncrasies of this incredible place are compressed into a single year. Please forgive me for not allotting equal attention to all of the months or to all of the towns and villages. Life, work and location dictate my ability, time and desire to photograph. Admittedly, I enjoy quiet times and remote places. So summer months and peopled places are least represented. Collecting these images took a little less than a couple of decades. Exposing them took a little more than a few minutes. Selecting them took almost forever.

As the years have passed, the opportunity to photograph pristine areas has diminished. Along the shores and marshes, the footprints we leave behind are no longer from feet but from foundations. Consequently, most of my photographs are taken in publicly or privately preserved places like the Cape Cod National Seashore, state and town parks, beaches, landings and conservation areas. Sometimes, I sadly joke that the day may come when I will have to discard my wide-angle lenses to avoid man's imprint on our coast line.

Unlike the granite ridge that guards the coast of Maine, only sand bars and barrier beaches protect our shore from devastating storms. We continually construct revetments and walls to stave off the inevitable. Until recently, nature's fury was the only force to be feared. Now a greater, more insidious threat sits not on the horizon, but under our feet. It is us. It is everything we do and everything we leave behind. There are too many of us in too fragile an area. We spend much more time and money developing land than preserving it. Our pollutants and waste compromise the water quality of our aquifers, ponds, bays and estuaries. Congestion aggravates our lives. We are all asking the same questions. *Can we save what's left? Can we restore what's lost?*

Maybe, maybe not. It all depends upon our commitment to protect the environment that nourishes the quality of our lives. We need to create and respect laws that limit the negative effects of over-development. We need to preserve and procure open space. With volunteered time and generous donations of land and money, it may still be possible to save and restore the health and beauty of the Cape and Islands. Hopefully, this magnificent place will inspire you to help as much as it has inspired me to create.

PHOTOGRAPHER'S STATEMENT

Like most photographers, I began my career at the age of three months when my mother accidentally dropped her camera on me. The lens left a circular impression in my forehead that now looks like an abandoned third eye. The impact on what must have been my *photo lobe* precipitated an extraordinary chain of events. Though a little dazed, and I still remember the moment to this day, I picked up the camera in my crib and started shooting. At four months of age, I began speaking what seemed to my mother to be unintelligible gibberish – words like aperture, shutter speed and hyper focal point. By eight months, my first two bodies of work were hanging in prestigious Midwest art galleries. My first show consisted of ten mind-altering abstracts of spilt milk and cereal on colorful plastic trays. Shortly thereafter, I received an NEA grant to document diaper rash in Lake County, Ohio...

Don't I wish it were true.

Truthfully, I am photographically challenged – an unschooled, self-taught heathen with no formal training or guidance. However, I must admit to taking a photography class in 10th grade – black and white, of course. Much later, in 1984, I applied to one of Ansel Adams' summer workshops. The day I received the invitation, Ansel Adams died. The world works in mysterious ways. I never really understood this message. Fortunately, I really enjoyed photographing and forged ahead undaunted.

My photographic pursuit really began in 1981, at age 36, when my wife and I decided our workaholic life style needed some equilibrium. Lynne and I had worked 7 days a week for ten years to insure the success of our gallery, *Yankee Ingenuity*.

We spent our days, nights and weekends finding and refinishing antiques. I learned clock repair, woodworking, scrimshaw and stained glass. Lynne became a master at furniture refinishing, and an expert with grinding and polishing wheels as well as belt and finish sanders. Her brushwork was as flawless as her devotion.

One day we woke up and realized that we were not spending anytime outdoors. Though we lived and worked on Cape Cod, we were not enjoying its magnificent beauty. So we decided to change our focus, gradually left the world of antiques and started selling reproductions, art, crafts and photographs. Whenever the weather was decent or interesting we would spend our mornings and evenings before and after work exploring the Cape from Falmouth to Provincetown. When we took vacations, we went to exotic locales like Martha's Vineyard and Nantucket. For the next 13 years we traveled down every dirt road, canoed up every river and walked every trail the Cape and Islands had to offer.

While I photographed, Lynne would record my tech notes, read or write, dance, exercise or practice Tai Chi. Her energy was boundless, her strength extraordinary. She graciously helped me haul heavy photographic equipment to distant and remote places. Lynne was my partner, my soul mate in life and work, 24 hours a day for 26 years.

Then, at age 46, Lynne was diagnosed with terminal cancer. She accepted it like a saint, but fought it like a warrior. For two years, she endured the painful medicines of the West, pursued the transcendental philosophies of the East and ultimately found healing in her own spiritual being. Near the end Lynne confided she was content with her life and prepared for death. Though she may have been prepared, I was not. Her mother, Neva, a trained nurse, crossed the continent and moved in with us for the last six months. I soon discovered where Lynne acquired her compassion and strength. I felt doubly blessed by their presence. When Lynne fell into a coma, our best friends rallied to help. Margaret, Mary, Joan and Sharon took a week's personal time to stand vigil until Lynne passed away at 4:10 am, August 31, 1994, at age 48.

For the next two years, I photographed less than a dozen times. When you share a passion and a pastime for so long, it's difficult to do it alone. I had promised Lynne that I would finish the photography book we started and dedicate it to her. I never expected it would take me so long to recover and fulfill that promise. Until now, every attempt to work on the book has reduced me to tears. It's been ten years since we started the book and over seven years since I lost Lynne.

Fortunately for me, it's been nearly four years since I married Sharon, our friend who helped at Lynne's passing. Thanks to her, I'm photographing again on a regular basis. Sharon wisely encouraged me to photograph alone, in my own time. Though I resisted and wanted her company, it was necessary for me to photograph by myself. I had to rekindle my confidence and let go of past habits. I had to be in the moment. I had to record it. I had to share it. This is my passion.

Personally, I believe I must be in some uncertain way, quite possibly, if only slightly, but not harmfully, obsessed. Most assuredly, I'm not as obsessed as those people we all talk about when we say *he or she is truly obsessed.* No, not me, not ever. However, I must admit that I do seem to be obsessed with

photographing extraordinary moments – ones that are as brief as a beached wave, as ephemeral as fog, as illusive as a mermaid. I am drawn to images that are awe-inspiring, beautiful, meditative, peaceful, transcendental and whimsical. I need to share my respect for places that are sacred to the human condition – unspoiled land, marshes, beaches, ponds, bays and oceans. I need to tilt the scale away from the negative images of the nightly news – the human suffering, the environmental entropy.

What I most truly enjoy are the rare moments of being fully aware of everything within my viewfinder while simultaneously letting go of everything else. Emptying my mind is the most difficult part of photographing. Being obsessed is the easiest. Put simply, I follow my obsession. If I did not, I'd be battling the most stubborn foe I have ever met – me. So I just give in and photograph what I like.

That's the secret. The secret is that there is no secret – just photograph what you like. Follow your obsession. Maybe someone else will share your obsession. If so, you will have connected. If not, you can always rationalize that those with whom you don't connect are simply *obsessionally* challenged. Gradually, if your obsession is properly nourished, it will grow, flourish and someday possibly bring about world peace, or luckier still, you might be pursued by adoring *groupies* seeking autographs and special favors. In spite of what you may have read, heard or fantasized, the latter does not usually happen to landscape photographers.

Of course, being obsessed has its responsibilities. First, you must make time for photographing. Second, you have to learn to shift gears from one obsession to another without stripping your clutch. The transition from workaholic to *photographaholic* is always challenging. The reverse is even more difficult. Third, you have to mortgage the house to buy the best gear to satisfy your particular obsession. Fourth, you have to read and comprehend complex instruction manuals purposely confused in the translation from Swedish and Japanese. Fifth, you have to really like backpacking tons of photographic gadgetry. Obviously, the more weight you carry, the more professional you must be. My gear weighs forty-seven pounds. This means that I must be a better photographer than the amateur who carries only thirty pounds, but not quite as good as the professional who can pack up to sixty pounds. Of course, it must be understood that there is no handicap factor for the gear to body weight ratio. Just because you might be small does not mean you can get away with carrying less equipment. Last, to be truly obsessed, you must learn to become one with foul weather, irritating insects and oblivious bipeds who walk right into your picture just at the moment of exposure.

On the plus side, once you have acquired all this paraphernalia and are decked out in appropriate photographic attire, someone very close to you may remark that she thinks you look pretty sexy in rubber hip boots. It can happen. I know.

Seriously, as photographers or simply lovers of the Cape and Islands, we have only one responsibility – protect what we respect. The most beautiful places are the most fragile and endangered because everyone wants to see and experience them. Preserving them means protecting the environment. Whether we live here or visit here, we must be aware that even though our impact on the coast seems as benign as the crash of one wave, our combined and prolonged presence can be just as lethal as the relentless pounding of a nor'easter. It is wishful thinking to believe we cannot destroy these lands or the ocean that surrounds them. It is a delusion to believe we can afford the cost to restore what will be permanently polluted or lost. It would be best if we adhered to the old adage about leaving only footprints, preferably only on the trails, not in the beach grass or in someone else's back yard.

So go forth with loaded camera, photograph what inspires you and share your obsession.

Photographing the porch facade of the dune shack (page 93) proved to be a challenge. I wanted to create an intimate relationship between the shack and the dunes. To do so required positioning the camera in front of the deck about ten feet above the bottom of a gully. Using found objects stowed beneath the shack, I lashed and wedged together a sturdy scaffolding to support me and my tripod. The materials included aluminum and wooden ladders, landscaping ties, driftwood boards and branches, cinder blocks, bungee cords and clothes line. Constructing, photographing and de-constructing took a little less than two hours. My wife, Sharon, immortalized my obsession in this photograph.

COASTAL EFFECTS

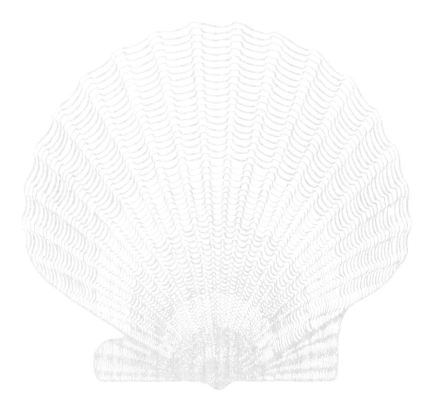

JANUARY

Cape Cod Bay, North Truro   BORDERING THE BAY   January 1, 1992 – 4:35 pm

Rock Harbor, Orleans   ALLUVIAL ILLUSION   January 3, 1983 – 9:00 am

Province Lands, Provincetown   WIND ETCHED DUNE   January 7, 1990 – 1:05 pm

Morris Island, Chatham   MUSSEL BEACH   January 8, 1990 – 3:10 pm

West Dennis   BITTERSWEET WINDOW   January 14, 1991 – 3:05 pm

Provincetown   LONG POINT LIGHT   January 16, 1990 – 4:17 pm

Stage Harbor Light, Chatham

MOORED IN ICE

January 17, 1988 – 4:35 pm

SANDLOCKED

The day before Halloween in 1991, a huge nor'easter, now known as *The Perfect Storm,* cut off the forearm of Cape Cod. Blowing out a 100 feet of dune at Ballston Beach, the Atlantic Ocean surged across Truro flowing down the Pamet River to its mouth in Cape Cod Bay. Fortunately, the headwater marsh vegetation was dormant, so most of it recovered, in spite of being covered by tons of dispersed sand and seven feet of saltwater. The breach, visible in the distance just above the porch roof, eventually healed and has not been washed over since.

Though a dozen beach camps and some boats in Chatham were destroyed, this 100 year old cottage, literally buried into the backside of a dune, was unharmed by the 60 to 80 mile an hour winds that haunted the Cape for three days. It may look like storm damage, but the sand piled up around the house is the result of accretion. For many years, winds whipping off the top of seaward dunes carried the sand grain by grain and deposited it inch by inch against the eastward walls. This process of shifting sands is most prevalent in Provincetown where snow plows have to push the sand off the roads after windy storms. The planting of beach grass and limiting access to critical areas has helped significantly in controlling the westward migration of the dunes. During these ferocious storms, projectile sand stings the flesh and severely sandblasts windows and automobile paint.

It was sandblasted and seaweed-plastered windows that kept the inhabitants of this cottage from witnessing the ocean breaking through the barrier dune. During an obviously restless night, they were awakened by wind-blown sea foam seeping through their window moldings and floating around the upstairs bedroom. The next day, after the storm had subsided, they ventured outside to discover the neighboring dune destroyed and several feet of sea foam congealed around the house. Since then the house has been lifted and now rests on a sturdy block foundation.

I will never forget this storm because it ripped a 21-foot sailboat from its mooring, floated it across a state highway and dumped it into my driveway. While shoveling seaweed and debris away from my mailbox, I was interviewed by a Boston television crew, appeared on the evening news and indulged in 15 seconds, unfortunately not minutes, of fame that everyone is supposed to experience in his lifetime.

More information about the *Great Gale of '91* is available from my source articles in the Friday, November 1, 1991 edition of *The Cape Codder* written by John LoDico and Joyce Johnson.

Ballston Beach, Truro   SANDLOCKED   January 31, 1993 – 1:15 pm

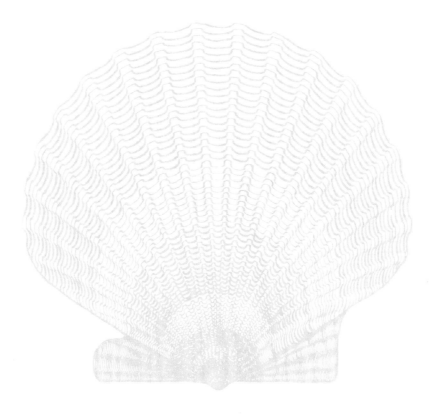

FEBRUARY

Ridgevale Beach, West Chatham   HERON AT COCKLE COVE   February 1, 1984 – 10:00 am

24

Buck's Creek, West Chatham   SAND HOOK   February 2, 1997 – 4:50 pm

25

Provincetown · OLD RELIABLE FISH HOUSE PIER · February 4, 1991 – 4:29 pm

West Dennis   SWINGLESS   February 8, 1991 – 9:35 am

27

Province Lands, Provincetown   NATURAL CRANBERRY BOG   February 12, 1990 – 3:15 pm

ATLANTIC WHITE CEDAR SWAMP

A little over a mile long, the Atlantic White Cedar Swamp Trail is my personal favorite and one of the most interesting on the Cape. Located in a depression created by a glacial chunk of ice, the swamp is just west of a windy bluff in Wellfleet at the Cape Cod National Seashore's Marconi station site. The trail begins in a wind-stunted thicket of gnarled oak and scrubby pine that gradually descends into a shaded forest. At the bottom of the trail where the swamp begins, a boardwalk guides you into a natural cathedral of weathered cedar trees. A lush green carpet of moss absorbs even the sound of the wind. The silence is remarkable and seems appropriate for a sylvan sanctuary. The dead tree snags take on anthropomorphic features that resemble intricately carved totems in an ancient sacred place. Here is where I photographed the dedication portrait of Lynne.

The Atlantic White Cedar tree is highly valued for its resistance to decay. The first European settlers of the new world used it for everything from house construction to fence posts. Eventually, all of the original forests were depleted and now, most of the cedar lumber comes from the maritime provinces of Canada where it is farmed as a renewable resource.

In coastal areas, the Atlantic White Cedar is traditionally used for shingling a house or constructing a stockade fence. Without paint or maintenance, it will last about 20 years, a little more if pickled by salty air and a little less if dampened in shade and subjected to mold. The classic weathered gray color is caused by prolonged exposure to sunlight. Depending upon the amount of sun exposure, the process takes 6 to 24 months. Old-time Cape Codders are always bemused by the newcomers who stain their shingles gray because the natural weathering process is uneven and takes too long.

On the Cape, everyone welcomes fresh snowfall because it's an infrequent visitor that doesn't stay very long. The pristine snow in this photograph melted in a few days. In northern Ohio, where I grew up, the *lake effect* kept snow on the ground all winter until its surface turned black from fossil fuel emissions. In Ohio, we couldn't wait for spring. On the Cape, there really isn't a true spring season. We usually have a very mild winter that lasts until some unspecified time in early June when, in one day, it suddenly turns to summer. The lackluster spring is more than made up for by the extended summer which sometimes lasts well into September and is followed by a gorgeous autumn. Contrary to wishful thinking, the weather is controlled by the Gulf Stream, not the Chamber of Commerce.

Marconi Station, Wellfleet   ATLANTIC WHITE CEDAR SWAMP   February 26, 1990 – 1:30 pm

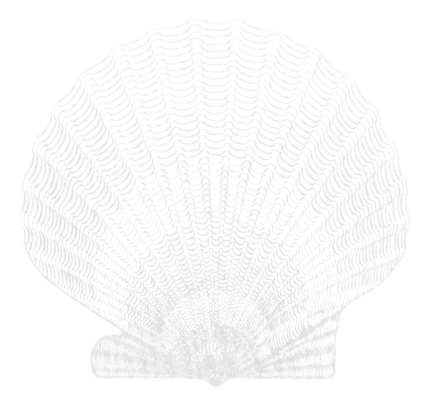

MARCH

Cape Cod Bay, North Truro   WHITE COTTAGES   March 21, 1992 – 3:30 pm

Province Lands, Provincetown   HERRING COVE DUNES   March 23, 1992 – 5:00 pm

Truro   PAMET HARBOR SUNSET   March 25, 1999 – 6:00 pm

Sandwich Harbor   BREAKWATER   March 26, 1995 – 2:05 pm

Cape Cod Bay, Dennis   QUIVETT NECK BEACH   March 29, 1999 – 5:50 pm

THE ELDIA

On March 29, 1984, blown off course by a fierce nor'easter packing up to 80 mile an hour winds, the *ELDIA*, a 471-foot Maltese freighter desperately dragging its anchors, was forced aground and embedded in soft sand near the shoreline just south of the Nauset Beach parking lot in East Orleans. Though knocked to the floor by the jolt of the grounding, the 23 crewmembers were unharmed and safely rescued by a Coast Guard helicopter that battled 60 mile an hour gusts. While hovering ten feet above the ships masts, the helicopter hoisted the crew in three trips from a rocking ship pounded by 20-foot seas.

Though the ELDIA's hull suffered a small crack, the 140,000 gallons of operational diesel fuel were safely pumped ashore into tanker trucks. Surprisingly and ironically, the only ecological damage done was by an estimated 30,000 sightseers who trampled the beach grass getting to the site of the grounding. Ultimately, the hull was patched and the vessel was returned to the sea on a high tide. Thanks to the valiant efforts of the Coast Guard and generous assistance of local residents, a near-tragedy was turned into a heroic rescue. More about this event can be found in my source – an April 3, 1984 front page article in the *Cape Codder* written by Greg O'Brien and John Gaffney

The sand bars off the coast of the Cape are tricky to navigate in good weather and treacherous in violent storms. According to William P. Quinn, in his book *Shipwrecks Around Cape Cod*, thousands of ships have been lost off the Cape since the first documented shipwreck in 1626. The *SPARROWHAWK*, carrying passengers from England to Virginia, was caught in a nor'easter and went aground on Nauset Beach. The 20 or so crew and passengers survived but had to spend the winter in Plymouth before continuing their journey. Coincidentally, they met their misfortune less than one hundred yards from the ELDIA's grounding.

Also, on page 109, I photographed the ribs remaining from the shipwreck of the *JOHN S. PARKER*, a British schooner that wrecked in Nauset Inlet in 1901. Her crew of six and part of the cargo of lumber were saved. During a conversation with Mr. Quinn, I learned that the ribs are exposed periodically. Because of prevailing winds, currents and storms, the remains suddenly appear and then disappear for years. They were uncovered again three years after I photographed them and, to the best of my knowledge, have not surfaced since.

Nauset Beach, East Orleans   ELDIA, THE MORNING AFTER   March 30, 1984 – 7:00 am

APRIL

Outermost Harbor Inlet, Chatham

CHATHAM LIGHT

April 10, 1988 – 1:30 pm

SHUCKED SHELLS

There is no morsel of meat sweeter or more succulent than the pure white muscle of an Atlantic Bay Scallop. This huge hill of discarded scallop shells is a testament to their tantalizing taste. Typical of Yankee ingenuity, nothing is wasted in the harvesting of shellfish. Most of these shucked shells will end up in a local driveway, crushed and compacted, to cover the dirt and keep down the dust. Many will be baby-oiled for shell collections, varnished or painted for Christmas tree lights and ornaments, polished and precious metal-plated for jewelry, hot glued and fabricated into sailors valentines, wall wreaths and silly souvenir sculptures. A few will become impromptu ash trays for those who have not yet kicked the habit.

Since I photographed this pile of shells, the Bay Scallop catch has diminished significantly. On the Cape, scallop shell beds that once produced thousands of bushels no longer provide even a single specimen. According to data from the Division of Marine Fisheries, most of the early 1980s averaged over a million pounds of Bay Scallops for each yearly harvest on the Cape and Islands combined. By 1990, when I photographed these shells, the catch was barely over half a million pounds. Since then even the 1990 amount has never been equaled. Unlike the fishing industry, over-harvesting is not the problem. The cause is human habitation. Massive amounts of nitrogen leaching from old and state-of-the-art septic systems have migrated into our coastal waters and killed off the eelgrass. The great beds of eelgrass that once were the nurseries for seed scallops are now barren bottoms of sand and mud.

The possible demise of Bay Scallops is only part of the problem. Too much nitrogen, though not particularly harmful to humans, is the primary cause of algae blooms in coastal bays and estuaries. Besides smelling awful, decomposing algae sucks oxygen from the water and causes massive fish kills. Reversing the destructive effects of nitrogen loading will be difficult and expensive. Limiting land development, upgrading to denitrifying septic systems and sewering sensitive coastline areas are some of the possible solutions. However, if we do not address this situation soon, the sweet taste of Bay Scallops and other threatened fish species may become only a memory.

Shawkemo Hills, Nantucket   SHUCKED SHELLS   April 24, 1990 – 11:30 am

42

Mitchell River, Chatham   TRAP SHACK   April 24, 1988 – 2:00 pm

Rock Harbor, Orleans   ALL MEAT, NO FILLER   April 29, 1991 – 1:58 pm

Breakwater Landing, Brewster   FOG BANK   April 29, 1986 – 6:45 pm

Mayflower Heights, Provincetown   CLOSE ENCOUNTER OF THE BRIEF KIND   April 30, 1982 – 5:30 pm

MAY

Coast Guard Beach, Eastham   GREAT ATLANTIC SURF BIRD   May 7, 1989 – 2:30 pm

Boatmeadow Beach, Eastham   BUDDING BLACK LOCUST   May 18, 1989 – 7:30 pm

Yarmouth Port

PAPER MONEY IN SLOT

May 21, 1989 – 1:00 pm

Mill Pond, Brewster   HERRING RUN   May 23, 1987 – 9:30 am

53

JUNE

Lieutenant Island, Wellfleet   MOORED IN PEACE   June 1, 1984 – 11:00 am

Stage Harbor, Chatham   FISHERMAN'S DORY   June 2, 1988 – 8:00 pm

AQUINNAH CLIFFS

The Aquinnah Cliffs, formerly known as the Gay Head Cliffs, are a mile long and 150 feet high. I have photographed them many times, but I think this view best represents the remarkable variegation of colors in the ancient clay deposits. Preserved as a National Landmark, the 100 million year old striated sediments of the cliffs were forced to the surface by advancing glaciers about 12,000 years ago. Diminished by pounding waves and heavy rains that sometimes tint the surf red, the heavily eroded cliffs have been intricately carved into an elaborate natural sculpture of incredible beauty.

The Wampanoag have lived in Aquinnah, *place under the hill,* for thousands of years and consider the cliffs to be a sacred place. Oral history credits the creation of Neope, *land amid the waters,* (Martha's Vineyard) to a legendary, benevolent giant named Moshup. While journeying to the Atlantic coast, Moshup became very tired and dragged his massive foot across the land which created a long depression in the ground that eventually filled with water and separated what is now known as Martha's Vineyard from the mainland. He settled in Aquinnah, at the southwestern end of the island, where he caught whales barehanded and slaughtered them on the beach. According to the Moshup legend, the red-colored clay in the cliffs was caused by the whales' blood. Moshup shared his catch and wisdom with the Wampanoag people, who have revered him as a great provider and teacher. He taught the tribal members how to fish, farm and care for the land they shared with all of the creatures of the earth.

Out of 3400 acres of ancestral land on Aquinnah, 477 acres are still owned and protected communally by the Wampanoag Aquinnah Tribe. Thousands of years before European explorers discovered America, the Wampanoag of Neope lived in perfect partnership with their environment. Their civilization respected the resources of the land and water and always made sure enough would be left for future generations. For making functional and beautiful cooking pots, only the clay that was needed was removed from the sacred colored cliffs. Crop rotation and animal husbandry were common knowledge. Even today, fertilizers and pesticides are not used in their cranberry bogs. Menemsha Pond, covering 640 acres, is so clean that the Environmental Protection Agency has classified it as *pristine* – a testament to the dedication of their stewardship.

When asked to describe the culture of the Wampanoag, *People of the First Light,* Ramona Peters, a Mashpee Wampanoag, replied: *We name ourselves after the land we live with. Because, not only are we breathing in, we are also drinking from the water that is flavored by that very land. Whatever is deposited in the soil is in the water is in us. So we are all one thing, and we name ourselves after the place that is our nurturing, that sustains our life.*

More information about Aquinnah and the Wampanoag people is available on the tribal website – *www.wampanoagtribe.net.*

Aquinnah, Martha's Vineyard

AQUINNAH CLIFFS

June 8, 2000 – 12:25 pm

Atlantic Ocean, Wellfleet

WHITE CREST BEACH

June 9, 1986 – 3:10 pm

Moshup Beach, Aquinnah, Martha's Vineyard

EVENING TRANQUILITY

June 15, 1990 – 6:40 pm

Aquinnah, Martha's Vineyard   GAY HEAD LIGHT   June 15, 1990 – 8:00 pm

Aquinnah, Martha's Vineyard   TEN MINUTES LATER   June 15, 1990 – 8:10 pm

Vineyard Haven, Martha's Vineyard

MISTY MORNING

June 17, 1990 – 7:10 am

Surfside, Nantucket

MIACOMET POND

June 22, 1995 – 8:00 pm

JULY

Stage Harbor, Chatham   PALETTE OF SAILBOATS   July 22, 1989 – 8:30 am

Linnell Landing, Brewster   RAIN ON THE HORIZON   July 23, 1993 – 8:10 pm

PURPLE LOOSESTRIFE

Though visually beautiful in mid-summer, Purple Loosestrife is a foreign plant imported from Europe that, because of its rapid and vigorous growth, now jeopardizes the survival of local marsh vegetation. Also threatened are the animals that need this native vegetation for food and habitat. Friends of mine who tried to cut and pull out the foreign flora from a neighboring marsh found their efforts frustrating and futile because of its intricately woven and densely matted root system.

Other invasive species threatening the Cape and Islands include Japanese knotwood, Honeysuckle, Phragmites australis, Multiflora rose, Oriental bittersweet and Autumn or Russian olive. I have successfully controlled and almost eradicated the Russian olive previously planted in my yard by an unknowing gardener, but my battle with bittersweet will be difficult and protracted.

Personally, I believe calling these plants *invasive species* may be a misnomer. Technically, we are the invasive species who introduced these plants to our habitat. Our desire to control or adorn the environment in seemingly harmless but unnatural ways has caught up with us in unforeseen but profoundly detrimental ways. Even the simple act of cultivating lawn grass that grows naturally in Kentucky has its adverse consequences. To survive in this coastal area, the imported grass requires lots of water and fertilizer, not to mention toxic chemicals to kill unwanted weeds. Potable water here is at a premium. Nitrogen in fertilizer, weedkillers and even manure leach into our coastal embayments and endanger our environment.

Cape Codders have taught me the many benefits of what is called a *Cape Cod lawn* – native grass that grows naturally, without watering, fertilizing or weed killing. The major benefit, besides the obvious protection of the environment, is the absence of maintenance. My Cape Cod lawn has survived even the worst droughts, needs infrequent mowing and is loved by birds that dine on the tasty weeds. Even without the aid of artificial feeding, my natural meadow is foraged by many feathered species that will not go near a manicured lawn. Admittedly, some birds can be a nuisance like the Sea Gull that landed on my grill and gulped down a chicken breast before I could shoo it away.

Great Salt Marsh, Sandwich   PURPLE LOOSESTRIFE   July 28, 1990 – 4:00 pm

AUGUST

Boatmeadow Beach, Eastham

CAT ON THE FLATS

August 4, 1996 – 10:20 am

SUN DIPPED

Sunrises, sunsets, moonrises, moonsets – I could retire today if someone had paid me minimum wage for all the hours I've stared at the horizon waiting for these magnificent moments to occur. I have planned many vacations so I could be in just the right spot at just the right time to witness, and hopefully, photograph these elusive events. Elusive, because even though they happen everyday, photographing them is totally dependent upon the weather.

The secret to photographing the sun as it rises or sets is having sufficient *cloud cover* to diminish the intensity of the sunlight. When you can look in the direction of the sun without seeing spots in your eyes, then the time is right. Caution: looking at the sun with the naked eye or through a viewfinder can cause severe and permanent eye damage. Also, be aware that through-the-lens light meters are fooled by direct sunlight entering the lens, especially if the sunlight is reflected in water. Adding one to one and a half stops of light to the meter reading will keep the image from being too dark. Bracketing the exposure in half-stop intervals will usually ensure at least one properly exposed image.

Patience is sometimes rewarded. Wait until the sun dips below the horizon to photograph the *half halo* that projects into the sky. Wait even longer, 10 to 40 minutes, to photograph the glorious *afterglow* that sometimes follows the sunset. When the sun rises or sets in a clear sky, photograph away from the sun. The hues of dawn and dusk are exquisite. Below the elbow of the Cape, we are blessed by geography that makes it possible to see sunrises and sunsets over the water in the same day. If the conditions are not good on one side of the Cape, a short drive to the other side might be more rewarding.

Moonrises and moonsets require precise planning. Generally, only one or two days out of each month are suitable for photographing a full moon rising or setting. In order to hold detail in the moon, so that you can see the craters, the light reflected by the moon needs to be close to the same value as the surrounding scene. This set of circumstances happens when the moon rises about 10 to 40 minutes before the sun sets, or when the moon sets about 10 to 40 minutes after the sun rises. Another element that enhances an image is water vapor and dust particles in the *atmosphere* - a delicate veil of sea fog or cirrus clouds will add color and texture. Not asking for too much, am I? The conjunction of all of these elements is a rare and wondrous experience.

Linnell Landing, Brewster   SUN DIPPED   August 5, 1986 – 7:00 pm

Duck Creek, Wellfleet   BOAT FOR SALE   August 10, 1984 – 9:30 am

Boatmeadow Marsh, Eastham   SUMMER MARSHMALLOWS   August 27, 1990 – 10:50 am

Stage Harbor, Chatham   NET AND TWINE SHED   August 28, 1988 – 9:30 am

SEPTEMBER

MacMillan Wharf, Provincetown   P'TOWN FISHING FLEET   September 3, 1985 – 7:00 pm

Nauset Beach, East Orleans   SUNRISE AFTER HURRICANE GLORIA   September 10, 1989 – 6:55 am

Rock Harbor, Eastham   WAVES OF GRASS   September 10, 1984 – 6:45 pm

Sipson Island, Pleasant Bay, Orleans   COASTAL FOG   September 11, 2000 – 11:10 am

Province Lands, Provincetown   C-SCAPE DUNE SHACK   September 20, 1993 – 5:15 pm

Wellfleet   THE FRONT PORCH   September 22, 1986 – 4:00 pm

AT THE BEACH

Nestled in the Province Lands dunes, the C-Scape Dune Shack is an hour's trek from civilization and a century's retreat from the new millennium. Offered by *The Provincetown Community Compact* as a *Retreat for Art and Healing,* the shack is available to the public by lottery for those who long for quiet, creative solitude. Just over one dune to the north is Race Point Beach and the Atlantic Ocean. To the east, west and south lie rolling hills of beach grass and stunted trees punctuated by barren slopes of wind-etched sand.

This photograph was taken one morning near the end of our week's stay at the shack. The only sounds we heard that week were the waves of the ocean and the squawks of darting birds. The only people we encountered were a few bass fisherman on the other side of the beach dune. Oh, and I almost forgot the bright yellow vintage sightseeing plane that flew overhead one afternoon while we were showering on the porch beneath one of those solar camping showers. Of course, at our age, it was probably more embarrassing for the sightseers than for us.

The only responsibilities we had were living without running water, electricity and the telephone. The only obligations we had were to rest, reflect and create. Sharon spent her days reading and watercoloring, while I hiked the trails and beach in search of photographic opportunities. We spent the evenings sitting on the porch, preparing dinner and talking endlessly in the warm glow of kerosene lamps. Time actually slowed down – a rare experience in this frenetic culture. We returned to our lives fulfilled and refreshed.

The cryptic note tacked to the doorframe by the previous occupant says it all – *At the beach.* We could have added a footnote – *It just doesn't get any better than this.* Our stay at the dune shack gave new meaning to the phrase *winning the lottery.*

Province Lands, Provincetown   AT THE BEACH   September 28, 1999 – 8:35 am

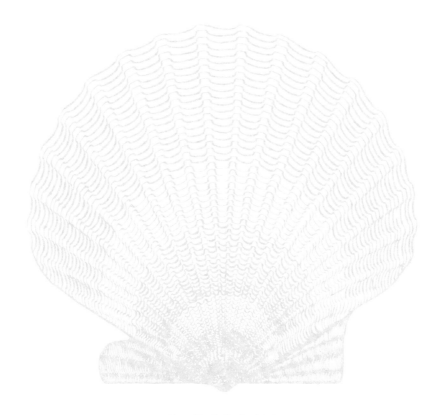

OCTOBER

Rock Harbor, Eastham   HARVEST MOON   October 4, 1990 – 6:35 am

Sankaty Point, Siasconet, Nantucket MARITIMELESS October 12, 1988 – 6:10 pm

Coskata, Nantucket   GREAT POINT LIGHT   October 13, 1988 – 6:00 pm

Coskata, Nantucket   GREAT POINT SUNSET   October 13, 1988 – 6:04 pm

Lieutenant Island, Wellfleet

OCTOBER MARSH

October 16, 1992 – 1:50 pm

Lieutenant Island Bridge, Wellfleet   FLOOD TIDE   October 17, 1993 – 1:20 pm

North Truro   AD INFINITUM   October 17, 1993 – 3:50 pm

Wellfleet   HIGH AND DRY   October 17, 1992 – 4:00 pm

Chatham

CHATHAM LIGHT & COAST GUARD STATION

October 18, 1987 – 4:25 pm

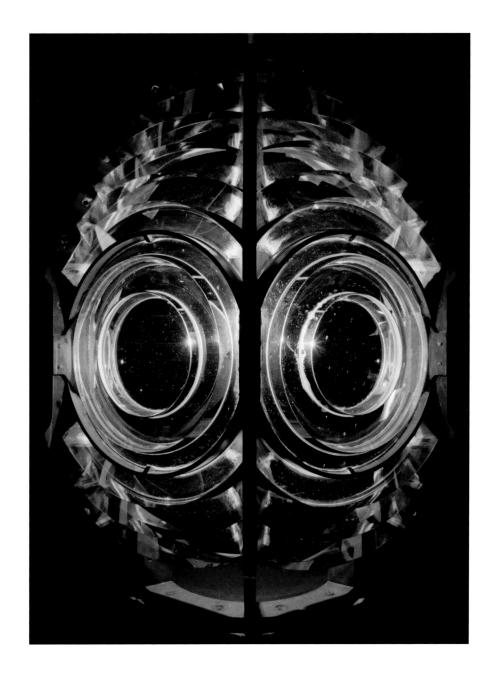

Atwood House Museum, Chatham   FRESNEL LIGHTHOUSE LENS   October 18, 1983 – 7:30 pm

Thumpertown Road Beach, Eastham

LOW TIDE

October 19, 1994 – 5:45 pm

Stage Harbor, Chatham A WAKE AT DAWN October 21, 1988 – 7:00 am

109

1901 Shipwreck, Nauset Beach, East Orleans   JOHN S. PARKER'S RIBS   October 22, 1990 – 7:05 am

South Orleans

PLEASANT BAY SUNRISE

October 23, 1989 – 6:20 am

North Tip, South Beach, Chatham

COBBLED SUNRISE

October 24, 1987 – 7:25 am

Stage Harbor, Chatham   COMPLEMENTARY BOW   October 25, 1989 – 5:45 pm

NOVEMBER

Coast Guard Beach, Eastham   SWEPT AWAY   November 2, 1997 – 2:00 pm

The Break, Chatham SOUTH BEACH SUNSET November 3, 1999 – 4:20 pm

CHANNEL MARKERS

The tidal flats of Cape Cod Bay are an amazing lunar landscape that draws the eye almost to the horizon at dead low tide. Small serpentine ridges of sand repeated ad infinitum in wave-like patterns flow horizontally along the curved coastline. The undulating landscape captures receding water in long graceful tidal pools that reflect the sky on calm days. Beachcombers love to walk these flats barefooted. The warm, shallow tidal pools soothe the feet and the soul. The only hazard is stepping on the sharp edge of a razor clam.

Boaters experience another hazard on these flats – finding the channel into Rock Harbor. Veering out of the channel on an outgoing tide could leave you grounded on the flats waiting hours for the tide to turn. Because standard channel marking buoys would be useless in these shallow waters, stationary tree saplings are planted in the meandering river channel that cuts across the flats. Local fishermen tell unsuspecting visitors that the channel markers are *clam trees* - hybrids which grow in salt water and produce delicious clams and quahogs. The truth is that they are not planted, but sunk into the sand with a gasoline powered water pump. Seawater forced through a hose held next to the base of the cut tree blows the sand away as the trunk is pushed a few feet down. The sand fills back in around the tree after the hose is pulled out.

Every year, during the first week of June, just before the boating season, a dozen or more pine trees are culled from the town forest and sunk into place by the harbormaster's crew and local charter boat captains. The process takes a few hours during low tide and also involves removing the broken stumps left from the previous year's crop. Hitting a submerged stump with a boat or prop can really ruin a good day of fishing. During most winters, enough ice forms on the bay to break or pull out all of the trees.

In my photograph, you will see round reflectors nailed to the trees as nighttime navigational aids. Recently, a few droll charter boat captains have posted additional aids to mariners. Some of the spurious signs I saw last year, placed there for those who believe clams grow on trees, read: BIKE PATH, COUNCIL ON AGING DOWNSTAIRS, SCHOOL BUS STOP, DANGEROUS INTERSECTION, YIELD FOR PEDESTRIANS, and DANGER – SOFT SAND.

Rock Harbor, Orleans   CHANNEL MARKERS   November 9, 1988 – 4:30 pm

Harding's Beach, West Chatham   THE CHATHAM LIGHTS   November 12, 1998 – 4:30 pm

Nantucket Sound, West Chatham   BUCK'S CREEK REFLECTION   November 13, 1996 – 4:30 pm

Pleasant Bay, South Orleans   DORY AT DUSK   November 15, 1998 – 4:30 pm

PEAKED HILLS

Snail Road is little more than a sandy footpath traversing the dunes to the Atlantic Ocean. At its highest point, where I took this photograph, it crosses Peaked Hills in the Province Lands of the Cape Cod National Seashore. In the distance are a few small dune shacks surrounded by what is now an uncommon expanse of undeveloped land. This beautiful open space is a welcoming oasis to both the senses and the soul. I was so inspired by this scene that every afternoon, for four days in a row, I drove an hour and hiked through rolling hills of soft sand to pursue this photograph. On the last day, after waiting an hour and a half, with very little daylight left, the sunlight suddenly streaked through a thick blanket of cumulus clouds and disappeared. The warm shaft of light illuminated the dunes for less than ten seconds, just enough time to expose a few frames of film.

Creating an image like *Peaked Hills* is only part of the pleasure of photographing. Scouting locations and experiencing the beauty of pristine places is its own reward. Over the past 20 years, I have enjoyed thousands of hours in pursuit of the illusive magic moment. This passion would have been short-lived had not been for the existence of the Cape Cod National Seashore. When it was designated in 1961, over 43,000 acres of land and 40 miles of beaches and marshes were permanently protected from development. In addition, thousands of acres have been preserved in private and public parks, land banks and trusts. If it were not for the generous and visionary people who gave time and money to save this paradise, most of it would have been denuded and developed into parking lots, malls and private residences.

Unfortunately, the hard work is still ahead of us. Purchasing open space for the health of our environment and the welfare of future generations has become our historical imperative. We are truly the last guardians of open space on the Cape and Islands. What we fail to save now will most surely be lost forever.

Snail Road, Provincetown   PEAKED HILLS   November 20, 2000 – 3:10 pm

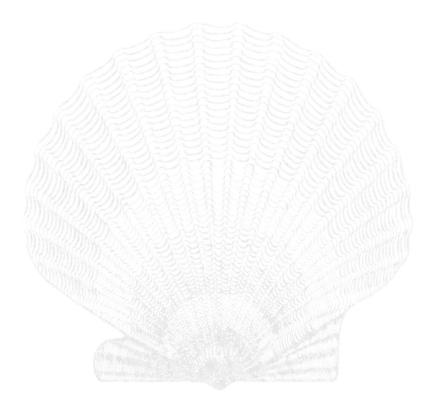

DECEMBER

Boathouse, North Chatham   A MOMENT OF REFLECTION   December 2, 1984 – 7:15 am

Chatham Harbor   SEA SNAG   December 18, 1997 – 4:25 pm

ALL THAT REMAINS

Walking the beach is always an adventure. It doesn't matter how many times I stroll the same stretch of sand, I discover something new every time. It could be a simple found object like a piece of colored beach glass that lives in my coat pocket for months. It could be a tumbled smooth rock shaped like a Valentine's heart or a piece of driftwood resembling a duck decoy that now resides on my patio. My favorite artifact is a gnarled chunk of milk white quartz with black eye socket depressions that looks exactly like a shrunken human skull and has now achieved the noble status of *paperweight.*

I've also found shipwreck ribs, a bottle with a note inside, a pilot whale skeleton, seal pups basking in the sun and dogfish sharks temporarily trapped in a tidal pool. For an hour one evening, I watched helplessly as a six-foot high sunfish caught on the flats in low tide battled its way to deep water. Some things are seen only once in a lifetime. A few years ago, I witnessed a peregrine falcon capture a small bird in mid-air. Swooping down at easily more than 100 miles an hour, the falcon struck the hapless bird with such great force that it exploded into a cloud of falling feathers.

One evening while walking Nauset Light Beach at dead low tide, I found a circular wall of mortared bricks, two feet high and a dozen feet in diameter. A trip to the Cape Cod National Seashore Visitors Center explained the mysterious object – the remaining foundation of one of the Three Sisters Lighthouses that had been moved back from the eroding cliffs in 1875. No one wants to believe the geologists when they report that the eastern shore of Cape Cod loses three feet a year to erosion. More than a century's loss of coastline was clearly confirmed when I discovered this foundation, once high on a cliff, now several hundred feet from the shore, buried in the sand, under water and exposed only infrequently by winter storms. I photographed it several times Christmas week before it disappeared beneath shifting sands and surging surf.

Nauset Light Beach, Eastham   ALL THAT REMAINS   December 24, 1999 – 4:20 pm

Pilgrim Lake, North Truro

MARSH AND DUNES

December 26, 1990 – 3:25 pm

Stage Harbor Light, Chatham   WINTER MOORING   December 30, 1989 – 10:15 am

Atlantic Ocean from Bearberry Hill, Truro

WINTERSCAPE

December 31, 1993 – 12:00 pm

Technique is a function of personal preference – something formulated by habit, desire and obsession. It's alchemy – a combination of science and magic - no two photographers use the same chemistry. I happen to be a detail junkie. When I view a framed print from across a room, I like the surprise of discovery as small objects and subtle elements are revealed during my approach. In landscape photography, fore and background details can be kept in focus only by using the smallest apertures. Accordingly, the shutter speed will be slow – too slow for hand holding (assuming the use of a slow-speed fine-grain film). Consequently, all of my photographs are taken from atop a tripod, the heaviest one I can carry. Though the set-up procedure is time consuming, the benefits are greater than just increased depth of field. Positioning the tripod forces me to find the best angle of view. Securing the camera frees my hands for ease of operation. Viewing from a fixed position offers me the stability and time to focus and fine-tune the composition. Using a slow shutter speed allows me to be creative with moving elements. In spite of all these wonderful advantages, I think it is still perfectly permissible to complain endlessly about carrying the heavy three-legged beast.

I use a medium format camera and 2-1/4 inch roll film. For me, it is an acceptable compromise between mobility and sharpness of image. Since lenses are the most important camera components for rendering fine detail and true color, I keep them shaded and never use filters. Well, almost never. On rare occasions, I will indulge in a polarizer. I use only single focal length lenses which are lighter, faster and have fewer pieces of glass than zoom lenses. All of my photographs are exposed with a shutter release cord and the mirror locked up to reduce unwanted camera vibration. Since bright sand and water can fool even the best light meter, I compensate and bracket my exposures in half-stop intervals whenever possible. If time permits, I expose the same scene in both positive and negative film, the former for offset printing and the latter for prints.

Being prepared is everything. I try to keep my equipment and film ready and with me at all times. Though I have scouted and returned to favorite locations for many years, some of my best photographs were taken without anticipation. However, I have lost innumerable images because my film was still in the fridge, my camera was in the closet, my battery was dead, my choice of location was wrong, my mind was cluttered, my heart was not in the mood or my chromes were processed in dirty chemistry. Agonizing over lost images is very painful, but in time, you learn to be thankful for just being there to witness the moment. Until then, along with complaining, swearing is also permissible.

The most difficult part of preparation is being in the right place at the right time. Several factors must be considered – location of sun, cycle of tides, and of course, the weather. I use *The Old Farmer's Almanac* to keep track of the known and flip a quarter for the unknown. Analyzing the combination of these elements determines where I want to be at a particular time. Sometimes I pre-visualize compositions in certain locations based upon the conjunction of anticipated conditions. It is absolutely extraordinary the way a scene is changed by high or low tide, clouds or clear sky, wind or calm, rain or fog. To help with the visualization, I use an age-old artist's tool – a frame.

138

From a piece of white plastic sized to fit in my rear pocket, I cut a window proportioned to my film format. By holding it in front of my eye, I can compose a scene to find the best angle. By moving it closer or further from my eye, I can quickly choose the correct lens – near means wide-angle, far means telephoto. After composing the image, I set up and wait for the right moment, or on many occasions, note the conditions that would be ideal and return another time. Consequently, I do much more looking than shooting.

When I do release the shutter, it is climactic. It means that I have documented a unique moment in a real place. Unlike painters and digital artists, I do not want the advantage of manipulation. For me the challenge of straight photography is creating art from fluid moments and found subjects. The necessary requirements are a good eye, good lenses, a good printer and good luck. Often the satisfaction is discovering the extraordinary in the ordinary. Sometimes the thrill is recording the truly remarkable. Most times the reward is simply witnessing and sharing the experience.

EQUIPMENT

Camera:
Hasselblad 2000 FC/M with Meter Prism Finder PME

Interchangeable Film Backs:
A16 (1-5/8" x 2-5/32" image size)

Interchangeable Lenses:
Zeiss Distagon CF 40 mm f/4
Zeiss Distagon F 50 mm f/2.8
Zeiss Planar F 110 mm f/2
Zeiss Tele-Tessar F 250 mm f/4
Zeiss Mutar 2 x T* Teleconverter

Panorama Camera:
Fujica G617 with fixed lens EBC Fujinon SW 105 mm f/4
(2-5/32" x 6-19/32" image size)

Paraphernalia:
"Top Secret" gadgets and aids too numerous to list
and almost too heavy to lift

PHOTOGRAPHER'S NOTES

Page	Title	Camera	120 mm Film	Lens	Filter	Exposure	f/stop
2	Sandflats and Starfish	H	Kodak 6005	110 mm		1/30	f/16
13	Bordering the Bay	H	Fuji RFP	250 mm		3/4	f/16
14	Alluvial Illusion	B	Kodak 6014	40 mm		1/125	f/16
15	Wind Etched Dune	H	Fuji RFP	50 mm		1/30	f/16
16	Mussel Beach	H	Kodak 6005	40 mm		1/4	f/11
17	Bittersweet Window	H	Kodak 6005	250 mm		1/4-1/8	f/16
18	Long Point Light	H	Kodak 6005	50 mm		1/2-1/4	f/22
19	Moored in Ice	H	Fuji RFP	110 mm		1/8-1/15	f/16
21	Sandlocked	H	Kodak 6005	40 mm		1/8	f/22-f/16
23	Heron at Cockle Cove	B	Kodak 6014	250 mm		1/4	f/8
24	Sand Hook	H	Fuji RDP II	50 mm		1/8-1/15	f/16
25	Old Reliable Fish House Pier	H	Fuji RFP	250 mm		1/8	f/16
26	Swingless	H	Fuji RFP	40 mm		1/8-1/15	f/16
27	Natural Cranberry Bog	H	Fuji RFP	50 mm	polarizer	1/8	f/11
29	Atlantic White Cedar Swamp	H	Kodak 6005	40 mm		1/15	f/11
31	White Cottages	H	Kodak 6005	110 mm	UV	1/60-1/125	f/11
32	Herring Cove Dunes	H	Kodak 6005	50 mm		1/15-1/30	f/16
33	Pamet Harbor Sunset	H	Fuji RDP II	110 mm		1/4-1/8	f/16
34	Breakwater	H	Kodak 6005	50 mm		1/30-1/60	f/16
35	Quivett Neck Beach	H	Fuji RDP II	50 mm		1/2-1/4	f/22
37	Eldia, The Morning After	B	Kodak 6014	110 mm	UV	1/30	f/16
39	Chatham Light	H	Fuji RFP	250 mm	UV	1/500	f/8
41	Shucked Shells	H	Fuji RFP	50 mm		1/15/-1/30	f/16
42	Trap Shack	H	Fuji RFP	50 mm		1/8	f/16
43	All Meat, No Filler	H	Fuji RFP	110 mm		1/60-1/125	f/11
44	Fog Bank	H	Kodak 6017	250 mm		1/30	f/22-f/16
45	Close Encounter of the Brief Kind	B	Kodak 6014	110 mm		1/60	f/16
47	Great Atlantic Surf Bird	H	Kodak 6005	50 mm		1/125	f/11
49	Budding Black Locust	H	Fuji RFP	110 mm		1/4	f/16
50	Paper Money in Slot	H	Kodak 6005	50 mm		1/30-1/60	f/11
51	Herring Run	H	Fuji RDP	50 mm		1/2-1/4	f/22
53	Great Rhododendron	H	Kodak 6005	50 mm		1/4	f/16
55	Moored in Peace	H	Kodak 6017	250 mm		1 sec.	f/16
57	Fisherman's Dory	H	Fuji RFP	250 mm		1 sec.	f/22
59	Aquinnah Cliffs	H	Fuji NPS 160	40 mm	polarizer	1/8-1/15	f/22
60	White Crest Beach	F	Fuji RDP	105 mm	polarizer	1/8	f/32
62	Evening Tranquility	F	Fuji RDP	105 mm		1 sec.	f/45
64	Gay Head Light	H	Fuji RFP	250 mm		1/4-1/8	f/16
65	Ten Minutes Later	H	Fuji RFP	250 mm		1/2	f/16
66	Misty Morning	F	Kodak 6005	105 mm		1/4	f/32
69	Miacomet Pond	H	Fuji RDP II	50 mm		1/2-1/4	f/16
71	Palette of Sailboats	H	Kodak 6005	250 mm		1/4-1/8	f/32
73	Rain on the Horizon	H	Kodak 6005	50 mm		1/2	f/16

Abbreviations:
B = Bronica ETR-S
F = Fujica G 617
H = Hasselblad 2000 FC/M

Color Negative Film:
FUJI NPS160 = Fujicolor Portrait NPS 160
Kodak 6014 = Kodacolor II
Kodak 6094 = Kodacolor VR 100

Color Reversal Film:
FUJI RDP = Fujichrome 100 Professional D
FUJI RDP II = Fujichrome Provia 100 Professional RDP II
FUJI RFP = Fujichrome 50 Professional D

Kodak 6005 = Kodak Ektachrome 100 Plus Professional Film (EPP)
Kodak 6005 = Kodak Ektachrome 100 Plus Professional Film (EPP)
Kodak 6017 = Kodak Ektachrome 64 Professional
Kodak 6033 = Kodachrome 64 Professional Film (PKR)

Page	Title	Camera	120 mm Film	Lens	Filter	Exposure	f/stop
75	Purple Loosestrife	H	Fuji RFP	50 mm		1/60–1/125	f/11
77	Cat on the Flats	H	Kodak 6005	110 mm		1/60	f/16
79	Sun Dipped	H	Kodak 6094	250 mm		1/8	f/8
80	Boat For Sale	H	Kodak 6017	250 mm		1/30	f/32
81	Summer Marshmallows	H	Fuji RFP	50 mm	Polarizer	1/4–1/8	f/16
83	Net and Twine Shed	H	Kodak 6005	50 mm		1/250	f/11
85	P'Town Fishing Fleet	H	Kodak 6017	250 mm		1/60	f/8
86	Sunrise after Hurricane Gloria	H	Kodak 6005	50 mm		1/8	f/22
87	Waves of Grass	H	Kodak 6017	110 mm		1/2	f/16
89	Coastal Fog	H	Fuji RDP II	250 mm		1/30	f/32
90	C-Scape Dune Shack	H	Kodak 6005	110 mm		1/15–1/30	f/16
91	The Front Porch	H	Kodak 6017	110 mm	Polarizer	1/8	f/16
93	At the Beach	H	Fuji NPS160	50 mm		1/8	f/22
95	Harvest Moon	H	Kodak 6005	250 mm		1/4	f/11
97	Maritimeless	H	Fuji RFP	50 mm		3/4	f/8
98	Great Point Light	H	Fuji RFP	250 mm		3/4	f/16
99	Great Point Sunset	H	Fuji RFP	250 mm		1/8	f/11–f/8
100	October Marsh	H	Fuji RFP	110 mm		1/4	f/16
101	Flood Tide	H	Kodak 6005	50mm		1/60	f/11
102	Ad Infinitum	H	Kodak 6005	50 mm		1/15–1/30	f/11
103	High and Dry	H	Kodak 6005	50 mm		1/15	f/16
104	Chatham Light & Coast Guard Station	H	Kodak 6033	110 mm		1/125	f/11
105	Fresnel Lighthouse Lens	B	Kodak 6014	50 mm		3/4	f/22
106	Low Tide	F	Kodak 6005	105 mm		8 sec.	f/45–f/32
108	A Wake at Dawn	H	Kodak 6005	50 mm		3/4	f/16
109	John S. Parker's Ribs	H	Fuji RFP	50 mm		1/2	f/11
110	Pleasant Bay Sunrise	F	Kodak 6005	105 mm		1/2	f/45
112	Cobbled Sunrise	H	Kodak 6033	50 mm		1/15	f/16
113	Complementary Bow	H	Kodak 6005	250 mm		3 sec.	f/32–f/22
115	Swept Away	H	Kodak 6005	50 mm		1/30–1/60	f/22
117	South Beach Sunset	H	Fuji RDP II	50 mm		1/2	f/22
119	Channel Markers	H	Kodak 6005	110 mm		1/2	f/16
120	The Chatham Lights	H	Kodak 6005	250 mm		3/4	f/22
121	Buck's Creek Reflection	H	Fuji RDP II	50 mm		1/8	f/16
123	Dory at Dusk	H	Kodak 6005	50 mm		3/4	f/16
125	Peaked Hills	H	Fuji RDP II	50 mm		1/15	f/22
127	A Moment of Reflection	H	Kodak 6094	250 mm		1 sec.	f/32
129	Sea Snag	H	Fuji RDP II	50 mm		4 sec.	f/22
131	All That Remains	H	Fuji RDP II	50 mm		3/4	f/16
132	Marsh and Dunes	H	Fuji RFP	250 mm		1/8–1/15	f/11
133	Winter Morning	H	Kodak 6005	250 mm		1/8	f/22
134	Winterscape	F	Kodak 6005	105 mm		1/15	f/32
144	Scenic Overlook	B	Kodak 6014	110 mm		1/60–1/125	f/11

ACKNOWLEDGMENTS

Four years ago I married *Sharon Hayes.* Had she not been a close friend of Lynne's, I seriously doubt I would have survived the tragedy or completed this photography book. Sharon's sympathy and compassion were selfless and boundless. I was so much in love with Lynne before and after she died that no other woman would have understood or tolerated my profound and prolonged grief. Only a best friend, only someone who loved Lynne and me, could have weathered such an emotional storm. I now understand the human capacity for love is greater than I ever believed possible.

This book, which I had promised Lynne I would complete and dedicate to her, would never have been actualized without Sharon's generous help. Her encouragement, patience and love inspired me to get beyond the pain and begin to create again. Sharon graciously volunteered to become the production manager for the book and wholeheartedly researched designers and printers. She found the perfect pair for my idiosyncratic personality and hired them before I could formulate another excuse to postpone the project. Her remarkable business expertise made it possible for me to fund the book and maintain creative control. With patience and perseverance, Sharon successfully navigated the labyrinth of red tape involved in Library of Congress, ISBN and property release applications and forms. Through e-mails, phone calls and correspondence she was the conduit, facilitator and protector who proficiently moved the process along so I could concentrate on image selection, sequencing and writing.

Sharon was also my editor. Without her, who knows when anyone would ever have seen a comma or how many run-on passive voice sentences would have been strung in a row. There were some days when I wished I had never given her that red pen. Sharon was an honest, forthright and merciless *(oops)* editor who sent me back to re-write more times than I thought possible. However, I will be the first to admit the final draft was always a significant improvement and well worth what I called *the agony.*

The amount of time Sharon contributed to this project was incredible, especially when you consider she was simultaneously involved in her own business. I cannot thank her enough! I truly feel like the most fortunate man in the world to have loved Lynne for the first half of my life and now Sharon for the second half.

Life is a continuum of chapters coming to fruition in foundation blocks that build to a pinnacle like the construction of a pyramid. Everything that follows must rest on what came before. Acknowledging just the people who helped with this book would, at the same time, be ignoring all those who formed the base of my life's structure. Therefore, I must begin with my mother and father, Kay and Dan, who successfully survived my childhood and were always there when I needed them. My father funded my first business loan when most bankers would have just snickered at my proposal. For 23 years, my mother worked for me as my bookkeeper, until succumbing to cancer six weeks after Lynne died.

My first and only mentor, Earl Hensel, life-long director of Boy Scout Camp Stigwandish in Madison, Ohio, was my first employer. For six years, Earl befriended and taught me the practical skills needed to survive in the woods and the ethical skills required to live in a community. He is directly responsible for instilling in me the respect for the environment and the love for humanity that I still hold dear today.

Bob Korn, of Bob Korn Imaging in Orleans, Massachusetts, has been my photographic printer and friend for twenty years. Without his skill and nurturing, I never would have become a successful photographer. He is both a craftsman and teacher, who has shared with me his artistic understanding of color and extensive knowledge of the photographic process. Through his patient guidance, Bob has made me critically aware of what is possible and what is impossible with film and paper. In addition to printer, his title should also be photo guru and miracle worker.

I am truly indebted to my gallery manager, the incomparable Cristen Nichols, who for the past 14 years has made it possible for me to sneak out of work to photograph. Assisting us, and equally appreciated for all their help in covering for us during this book's creation is my excellent and extraordinary staff – Victoria Brown, Martje Bryce, Judy Lannon, Chaitra McCarty, Maria Montague, Leslie Morris, Diana Sanders, Eileen Varner and Nicolette Varner. Thanks also to Jenna Moore, our computer wizard.

Even a thundering thank you is not adequate enough to express my great appreciation for the inspired design work performed by Bert Ihlenfeld. Bert's intuitive creative input, meticulous attention to detail, instructional direction, affable tolerance and forthright critical evaluation of wacky ideas proposed by an eccentric, picayune photographer were a blessing to yours truly. His lightning response time in organizing and transmitting massive amounts of cyberspace material enabled us to complete this project in spite of three time zones and kept Sharon and me scrambling day and night just to keep up.

Another thunder-clapping thank you goes to David Gray Gardner, Kevin Broady and the exceptional staff at Gardner Lithograph whose scanning and printing skills are without equal. David's sincere respect for photography, genuine concern for an individual's interpretation of color and superb craftsmanship are evident on every page of this book. The process of creating this book has been a very meaningful and significant building block in the pyramid of my life. I am profoundly grateful to the loving, generous and gifted people who helped me carve and lift this precious stone into place.

COASTAL EFFECTS
Cape Cod, Martha's Vineyard & Nantucket

First Edition 2002
Printed in the United States of America
Photographs and Essays © 2002 Jon Vaughan

Library of Congress Control Number 2002103087
ISBN 0-9718932-0-9

Designed by Bert J. Ihlenfeld, Pacific Grove, California
Printed on 100 lb Vintage Gloss Book by
Gardner Lithograph, Buena Park, California
Bound by Acme Bookbinding, Charlestown, Massachusetts

Published and distributed by
Yankee Ingenuity
525 Main Street, Chatham, MA 02633
(888) 945-9123
yankee-ingenuity.com

Lynne, Lighthouse Beach, Chatham

SCENIC OVERLOOK

June 13, 1983 – 11:15 am